Nelson Spelling

Pupil Book 6

OXFORD
UNIVERSITY PRESS

Book 6 Scope and Sequence

Unit	Pupil Book Focus	Pupil Book Extra	Pupil Book Extension	Resource Book Focus	Resource Book Extension
1	**simple plurals** finding target words	identifying *s/es/ies* endings	understanding irregular plural forms	picture matching; writing plurals	understanding spelling rules; writing plurals
2	**tricky plurals** finding target words	creating *f/fe* plurals	understanding *o* endings; identifying plural forms	picture matching; writing plurals	understanding spelling rules; writing plurals
3	**using prefixes** adding prefixes rule	understanding English origin prefixes	alphabetical ordering	adding prefixes	identifying antonyms; writing sentences
4	**using suffixes** finding target words; word sums	identifying *e* + suffix rules	using *e* ending + able/ible	using *e* + *ing*; cloze activity	understanding suffix rules
5	**using suffixes** finding target words; adding *ed*	identifying *y* ending + suffix	identifying single or double; dictionary work	using *y* + ed; cloze activity	using *y* + other suffixes
6	**maths and science words** finding target words	correcting common errors	matching definitions; dictionary work	adding missing letters	completing and making a crossword
7	**ph** completing a wordsearch; sentence writing	choosing *ph* or *f*	identifying Greek origins; dictionary words	word building; picture matching	adding missing letters; sorting words by silent letter; writing sentences
8	**tricky words 1** identifying common errors	identifying key letter omissions	correcting double-letter common errors	adding missing letters; sorting words by silent letter	editing activity
9	**word roots** identifying word roots	writing definitions of selected roots	identifying roots and Latin and Greek roots	identifying Latin and Greek roots	using a dictionary to write definitions
10	**word origins** identifying recent word imports	identifying word sources	sorting Italian roots	picture matching	identifying French word origins
11	**unstressed letters** completing a crossword	identifying unstressed vowels and consonants	working with syllables and unstressed vowels	finding unstressed letters	identifying syllables
12	**tricky words 2** completing a wordsearch	completing double letter quiz	correcting common errors	identifying *double letters* and *ough* words	writing definitions; marking a spelling test
13	**geography and history words** finding target words	correcting common history errors	matching words with definitions; dictionary work	adding missing letters	completing and making a crossword

The darker cells introduce statutory material for this year group in the National Curriculum for England.
The paler cells denote revision of a topic covered in previous years.

Unit	Pupil Book Focus	Pupil Book Extra	Pupil Book Extension	Resource Book Focus	Resource Book Extension
14	**ent ence ant ance** cloze activity	matching adjectives and nouns	making adverbs; writing phrases	completing a crossword; writing sentences	cloze activity; using a dictionary to write definitions
15	**silent letters** letter associations	completing a crossword	identifying syllables; sentence writing	sorting silent letter words; picture matching	writing sentences; correcting common errors
16	**useful connectives** completing a wordsearch	identifying common connectives	connectives cloze activity; writing sentences	completing a wordsearch	writing sentences with compound connectives
17	**homophones and near homophones** finding target homophones	identifying near homophones	identifying noun and verb homophones	writing sentences with homophones	writing definitions
18	**er ar or endings** finding target words; sentence writing	cloze activity	alphabetical ordering	matching words and pictures with clues	cloze activity; using a dictionary to write definitions
19	**ery ary ory endings** completing a wordsearch	adding endings; identifying word roots	understanding plural forms of target word patterns	matching words and pictures; sorting words	word puzzle; writing definitions and word roots
20	**tricky words 3** vowel letter puzzle	finding root words	correcting common errors	letter patterns; adding suffixes	adding suffixes; writing sentences
21	**British English or American English?** identifying American and English spellings	identifying problem suffixes	correction activity	sorting words; writing sentences	identifying equivalent words; writing a letter
22	**a + double letters** finding target words	completing a wordsearch	identifying syllables	letter patterns; picture matching	checking spellings
23	**ie ei** identifying the 'i before e' rule	completing a *ie/ei* table	identifying different *ie/ei* sounds	picture matching; writing sentences	word quiz; completing words
24	**more unstressed vowels** target word quiz; sentence writing	identifying unstressed vowels	identifying syllables and unstressed vowels	finding unstressed vowels	identifying syllables and unstressed letters
25	**tricky words 4** picture quiz cloze activity	correcting common errors	correcting common errors with unstressed letters	picture matching	completing a table; writing sentences
26	**ICT words** finding target words	correcting common errors	understanding internet language	writing labels	writing definitions
27	**tricky words 5** matching words and contractions	correcting common errors with double letters	correcting common errors with omitted letters	word matching	completing and making crosswords
28	**using a dictionary** alphabetical ordering	finding information using a dictionary	using guide words	alphabetical order	using guide words

revisiting: simple plurals

When the star**s** come out the fox**es** are about!

Focus

Match a key word to each picture clue.
Underline the letters in each word that make it a plural noun.

1 _____   2 _____   3 _____

4 _____   5 _____   6 _____

7 _____   8 _____   9 _____

Remember, to make a noun plural we normally add **s**.

  teacher   teacher**s**

But if the noun ends with **s, x, ch** or **sh** we add **es**.

  bu<u>s</u>   bus**es**   fo<u>x</u>   fox**es**
  mat<u>ch</u>   match**es**   bus<u>h</u>   bush**es**

If a noun ends in **y**, we usually change the **y** to **i** and add **es**.

  countr<u>y</u>   countr**ies**

But if the letter before the **y** is a vowel, simply add **s**.

  d<u>ay</u>   day**s**

A Write the plural form of each of these nouns.

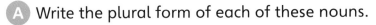

1 ash	2 pen	3 glass	4 monkey
5 party	6 display	7 donkey	8 shoe
9 puppy	10 box	11 watch	12 match

B When we make a plural verb singular (e.g. they talk, he talk**s**) we need to follow the same rules. Copy the chart and write four verbs in each column that follow these rules. One of each is done to help you.

+s		+es		+ies	
jump	jumps	push	pushes	hurry	hurries

Some nouns don't follow the simple rules. To make some nouns plural, several letters in the word need to be changed – or sometimes, none!

woman wom**e**n   child child**ren**   sheep **sheep**

Write the plural form of these nouns.

1 goose	2 mouse	3 cactus	4 ox
5 foot	6 crisis	7 grouse	8 tooth

Check your answers in a dictionary.

revisiting: tricky plurals

Where are the hippo**s** hiding?

Focus

Match a key word to each picture clue.
Underline the letters in each word that make it a plural noun.

1 _____   2 _____   3 _____

4 _____   5 _____   6 _____

7 _____   8 _____   9 _____

Remember, to make the plural form of nouns that end with **f** or **fe**, we usually change the **f** or **fe** to **v** and add **es**.

wol<u>f</u>   wol**ves**   wi<u>fe</u>   wi**ves**

A Write the plural form of each of these nouns that end with **f** or **fe**. Some follow the rule, but some do not.

1 used for cutting
2 keeps your neck warm
3 found along the coast
4 a married woman
5 leader of a group
6 large wild dog

B Check your answers in **A** and work out a rule for the words that are an exception to the main rule.

> Be careful! There are some important exceptions to this rule including belief/beliefs, reef/reefs and words ending in **ff**.

To make the plural form of most nouns that end in **o** we add **es**.

one potato   two potato**es**

A Write the plural form of these nouns.

1 mango
2 cargo
3 radio
4 logo
5 photo
6 soprano
7 shampoo
8 piano
9 volcano
10 cockatoo
11 cello
12 domino

> Abbreviations, music words and words ending in **oo** are exceptions and we add **s** to make them plural.

B Copy and complete this word puzzle.

clue	number of letters	first letter	plural noun
bouncing sound waves	6	e	
single-horned large African animal (abbreviation)	6	r	
fired from submarines	9	t	
long-legged pink bird	10	f	
wild Australian dog	7	d	

revisiting:
using
prefixes

Key Words

disappointed
dissatisfied
dissimilar

unsure
unnecessary
unnatural

overseas
overrule
overreact

impatient
immobile
immovable

Focus

The rule when adding a prefix is: just add it!
Don't change or miss out any letters.
   Example: un + sure = unsure

Sometimes, adding a prefix creates a double letter.
   Example: dis + satisfy = di<u>ss</u>atisfy

Bringing together the last letter of the prefix with the first letter of the word causes the double **s**. Don't be tempted to leave out an **s**.

A Add these prefixes to their roots, being careful to remember the rule.

1 dis	+ satisfy	service	jointed
	able	similar	solve
2 un	+ necessary	occupied	nerve
	numbered	natural	named
3 over	+ react	seas	rule
	ride	rated	run
4 im	+ possible	migrant	mortal
	modest	mature	movable

You will find a dictionary helpful for this exercise.

B Write a word that uses each of these prefixes and whose root begins with the same letter as the last letter of the prefix. Use each word in a sentence of your own to show what it means.

  1 mis   **2** inter   **3** pre   **4** re

Many prefixes used in English originally came from other languages, but some are English words and therefore easier to spell.

Example: **down**

downcast   **down**beat   **down**fall   **down**pour   **down**trodden

Remember, sometimes we use a hyphen when using a prefix:

over-hasty   over-confident   over-protective

A Write three words that begin with these prefixes.

1 out   2 under   3 super   4 up   5 be

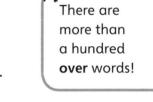

There are more than a hundred **over** words!

B There are a large number of words that have the prefix **over**.
How many can you think of? Write them in your book.

C Copy these groups of words.
Neatly underline the prefix in each word.
If you need to, use a dictionary to find the meaning of the words.
Write what you think the prefix means.

1 microchip   microfilm   microscope
2 forecast   foretell   foresee
3 antiseptic   antibiotic   antifreeze
4 submarine   subway   subsonic
5 precaution   prepare   preface

Arrange each group of words in alphabetical order.

1 antenatal   antecedent   anteroom
2 contrary   contraflow   contradiction   contravene   contralto
3 discharge   disappear   disagreement   disappointing   dissatisfied
4 international   interface   interval   intervene   interjection

revisiting:
using suffixes

care care**less** car**ing** care**ful**

Focus

A Match a key word ending in **ing** to each of these actions.

1 _____ 2 _____

3 _____ 4 _____

B Copy and complete these word sums in your book. Look at the words that you have just written in **A** to give you a clue about what happens to the final **e**.

1 slide + ing =   2 splice + ing =   3 crave + ing =

4 scrape + ing =   5 love + ing =   6 chase + ing =

To add a suffix when a word ends with **e**:

- drop the **e** if the suffix begins with a vowel
  wak<u>e</u> + **i**ng = waking
  sham<u>e</u> + **e**d = shamed
- keep the **e** if the suffix begins with a consonant
  wak<u>e</u> + **f**ul = wakeful
  sham<u>e</u> + **l**ess = shameless

Some exceptions to this rule include:

true	truly	argue	argument
due	duly		

> Suffixes beginning with a vowel are called **vowel suffixes** and those beginning with a consonant are called **consonant suffixes**.

Add these suffixes to each of the words. Write the new word that is formed.

1 package + ing = 2 place + ed = 3 manage + ment =
4 safe + ty = 5 combine + ation = 6 judge + ment =
7 relate + ion = 8 argue + ing = 9 imagine + ation =
10 share + ing = 11 care + less = 12 insure + ance =

Extension

When adding the vowel suffix **able** or **ible** to a word that ends with **e**, we nearly always drop the **e**. But there are some important exceptions!

> Americans sometimes keep the e where we drop it, such as **lovable/ loveable**.

A Complete these word sums. Use a dictionary to spot the four words in the group that must keep their final **e** when the vowel suffix is added.

1 value + able = 2 change + able = 3 cure + able =
4 believe + able = 5 peaceful + able = 6 recognise + able =
7 sense + ible = 8 desire + able = 9 notice + able =
10 response + ible = 11 love + able = 12 service + able =

B Work out and write down a rule to help you remember which words keep their final **e** when a vowel suffix is added.

revisiting: using suffixes

Focus

A Copy each of these verbs into your book. Next to each write the word with **ed** added. Remember to change the **y** to **i**.

worry

1 _____

carry

2 _____

bury

3 _____

marry

4 _____

hurry

5 _____

mutiny

6 _____

B Write three more words ending in **y** that follow the same rule.

To add a suffix when a word ends with **y** (where the **y** sounds like the **i** in t<u>i</u>n), you change the **y** to **i** and add the suffix.

ugly   ugl<u>iness</u>

A Add these suffixes to these words.

1 merry + ment   2 marry + age   3 crazy + est   4 funny + ly
5 naughty + ness 6 stormy + er   7 happy + ly   8 geology + cal
9 jolly + ty   10 necessary + ly 11 subsidy + sed 12 energy + sed
13 duty + ful   14 botany + cal   15 choosy + est   16 beauty + fully
17 happy + ness   18 gloomy + est   19 bounty + ful   20 melody + ous

B Find six other examples where **y** at the end of a word has been changed to **i** when the suffix has been added.

Extension

To add a suffix ending with **ll** to many words, we drop one **l**.

doubt + full = doubtful

If the root word also ends with **ll**, we sometimes delete one **l** from the word, as well as one from the suffix.

will + full = wilful

However, this is not a 'rule' as there are several exceptions, especially for words with a **ness** suffix.

stillness

A Join these together. Check your answers in a dictionary. Some are exceptions to the rule.

1 skill + full   2 thought + full 3 full + fill
4 full + ness   5 joy + full   6 fate + full
7 shrill + ness   8 hill + side   9 care + full

B Look in your dictionary and list the words that begin with the sound **all** (as in b**all**), such as **al**mighty.
Write a rule about what you notice.

maths and science words

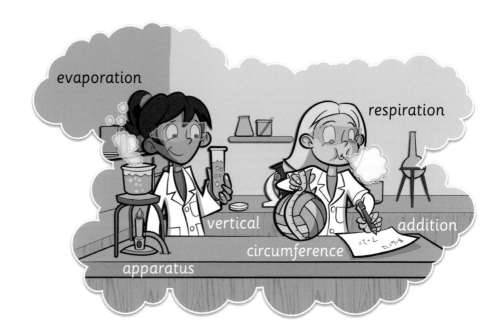

addition
subtraction
multiplication
division

parallel
horizontal
vertical
circumference

evaporation
condensation
respiration
apparatus
laboratory

Focus

Look at these pictures. Select and write a key word that matches each one.

1 _____

2 _____

3 _____

4 _____

5 _____

6 _____

7 _____

8 _____

9 _____

Extra

These maths words contain common misspellings.
Write them correctly in your book.

> When you have finished, check your answers in a dictionary.

1 adition
2 approximatly
3 centimeter
4 cercumfrence
5 horizontle
6 meashure
7 parralel
8 negitive
9 symetrical
10 virtical
11 volumn
12 wieght

Extension

A Match a word from the box to each of these scientific definitions.

> mammal   evaporate   dissolve   friction
> oxygen   vertebrate   condensation   digestion

1 to turn into vapour

2 one of the gases found in air, necessary for life

3 an animal with a backbone

4 absorbing food

5 to disappear when stirred in a liquid

6 caused when an object rubs against another

7 an animal that produces milk for its young

8 water formed from vapour

B Copy these words. Next to each one, write a simple definition. Use a dictionary to help you.

1 predator
2 perimeter
3 perpendicular
4 rhombus
5 isosceles
6 laboratory
7 parallelogram
8 respiration

ph

Key Words

graph

pheasant
phone
photo
physical

alphabet
dolphin
elephant

geography
microphone
pamphlet
sphere

Focus

A There are seven **ph** words hidden in the puzzle. Write them in your book.

a	p	v	l	n	t	x	m	b	g	p
k	l	m	l	c	h	g	r	a	p	h
e	l	e	p	h	a	n	t	e	h	e
m	r	p	h	o	n	e	d	f	o	a
t	s	p	a	m	p	h	l	e	t	s
w	x	i	b	o	p	q	n	u	o	a
a	z	v	e	d	o	l	p	h	i	n
j	b	y	t	p	r	u	p	f	z	t

B Write a sentence that uses two of the **ph** words from the puzzle box.

In most words **ph** sounds like **f**.
In this list of words every **ph** has been written as an **f**.
Write the words correctly in your book.

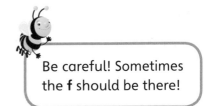

Be careful! Sometimes the **f** should be there!

1 alfabet   2 telefone   3 before   4 dolfin

5 sfere   6 geografy   7 pamflet   8 difficult

9 elefant   10 fotograf   11 triumf   12 fysical

Extension

Most words now used in English that start with, or contain, **ph** are words that came from the Greek language.
Examples: **phone**   *phone* is Greek for *voice* or *sound*
        graph   *graphein* is Greek for *writing*
        sphere   *sphairan* is Greek for *ball*
        photo   *photos* is Greek for *light*
        phobia   *phobos* is Greek for *fear*

A Sort the words in the box below into the lists according to their Greek root word.

autograph	stratosphere	microphone	atmosphere	claustrophobia
photograph	telephone	agoraphobia	graphic	hemisphere
paragraph	saxophone	telegraph	arachnophobia	

graph	sphere	phone	photo	phobia	spherical

B Choose four of the words and write a definition of each, knowing what you know about their Greek origins.

C Use a dictionary to help you find words beginning with **ph** that match these clues.

1 a small bottle for liquids
2 extraordinary; outstanding; remarkable
3 the collection of postage stamps
4 a string of words

Key Words

familiar
yacht
amateur
scissors
wrist
build
thistle
muscle
guitar
psychology
pneumatic
occupy
embarrassed
accommodation
exaggeration

Focus

Copy these words neatly into your book. Underline the letters you think someone might forget to put in.

guard	write	castle	muscle	guitar	wrong
scent	scissors	wrist	yacht	build	listen
whistle	wreck	biscuit	scenery	thistle	known

All of these words came into English from the Greek language.
They therefore have some slightly unexpected letter patterns.
One letter is omitted from each word. Write them correctly
in your book.

1 r__ubarb

2 r__eumatism

3 cata__rh

4 ast__ma

5 paral__se

6 __sychology

7 g__ography

8 g__ometry

9 archa__ology

10 autobiogra__hy

11 micr__scope

12 tel__scope

13 catastroph__

14 apostroph__

15 encyclop__edia

Extension

A Look carefully at these words.
All of the double consonants have been taken out.
Think carefully about which should be 'double letters'.
Write them correctly in your book.
Use a dictionary to check your final list.

1 exagerate   2 inocent   3 ocupy   4 ocasion   5 paralel

6 posesions   7 sudenes   8 woolen   9 adres   10 vacinate

B A pair of consonants is missing from each gap.
Copy the words, adding the missing letters.

1 a__o__odation   a place to live

2 a__ition   adding up

3 a__re__   name of where you live

4 co__i__ee   organised group of people

5 disa__oint   to let someone down

6 di__icult   not easy

7 emba__a__ed   feel awkward

8 qua__el   a disagreement

word roots

Focus

Roots are words or parts of words to which prefixes and suffixes can be added to make words from the same **word family**.

Copy these words. Next to each one write a key word that shares the same root, prefix or suffix.
The first one is done to help you.

1 biped   *bicycle*   2 microcosm   3 audition

4 transplant   5 zoology   6 export

7 aquatic   8 automatic   9 superbug

10 aeronautic   11 primate   12 preview

Roots can often provide a clue to the meaning of a word – and how to spell the word.
Example:
The <u>primary</u> school is the <u>first</u> school we attend (not counting nursery!).
The root **prima** comes from Latin and means *first*.

A Match each of these pairs of words with a root from the box below.

1 scribble manuscript
2 fluid fluent
3 duet duologue
4 thermometer speedometer
5 dialogue monologue
6 pedal pedestrian
7 aqueduct aquatic
8 decade decimal
9 geology geography

L = Latin
Gr = Greek

aqua (L) water   *scribere* (L) to write   *fluere* (L) to flow
deka (Gr) ten   *duo* (L) two   *logos* (Gr) word, speech
ge (Gr) the Earth   *metron* (Gr) measure   *pedis* (L) a foot

B Add another word that has the same root to each pair of words in **A**.

Extension

A Copy these words and underline the root of each word.
Use a dictionary to find the meaning of the words in each group then write what you think each root means.

1 pathetic   sympathy   apathy
2 portable   porter   transport
3 migrate   immigration   emigrate
4 octet   octagon   octopus
5 quadruplets   quadrangle   quad-bike

B Write a word that uses each of these Latin or Greek roots.

1 accidere (Latin for *to happen*)
2 centum (Latin for *hundred*)
3 facere (Latin for *to make*)
4 graphein (Greek for *to write*)
5 monos (Latin for *single*)
6 phone (Greek for *sound*)

word origins

kangaroo

cafe

pizza

easel

spaghetti

hoist
easel

burger
blizzard
okay

cafe
restaurant
ballet

kangaroo
dingo
kiwi

pyjamas
bungalow
verandah

Focus

English is a living and changing language. Here are words borrowed from languages in different parts of the world.

The Netherlands: *smuggle easel hoist sketch buoy*

France: *cafe restaurant boutique ballet banquet chauffeur*

India: *verandah bungalow pyjamas shampoo jungle*

America: *burger toboggan moose blizzard moccasins okay seafood*

Australasia: *kangaroo boomerang kiwi billabong dingo*

A Copy the table. Sort the key words in lists according to their area of origin.

The Netherlands	France	India	America	Australasia

B Add some more words to each list if you can.

The words we use today have come from different sources:

- from other countries   spaghetti (an Italian dish)
- from place names   wellingtons (from the boots worn by the
  or people's names   Duke of Wellington)
- from earlier languages   photograph (*photos* is Greek for *light*)
- from sounds   gurgle, cuckoo
- from abbreviations   mp3, jpeg

A Copy the table. Sort these words into lists according to their likely origin. Use an encyclopaedia, dictionary or online search engine to help you.

> August   splash   geology   sandwich   hiss   cardigan
> biro   thump   pizza   autobiography   cello   jangle
> hoover   sphere   boomerang   telephone   banquet

Onomatopoeia is the making of words from the sound they describe, such as 'pop'!

from other languages	from names	from old languages	from sounds	from abbreviations

B Try to add two more words of your own to each list.

These words have come into English from Italian.

> soprano   volcano   pizza   spaghetti   ravioli   concerto   alto
> piano   macaroni   opera   studio   pasta   confetti   umbrella

A 1 Write the words connected with food.
     2 Write the words connected with music.

B 1 Sort the words in the box into lists according to their last letter.
     2 What do you notice about the final letters of these Italian words that is different from most English words?

unstressed letters

family
boundary
raspberry
postpone
doctor
listener
different
separate
desperate
factory
dustbin
generally
generous
government
interesting

Focus

A Copy the word grid below. Using the key words, write the answers to the clues in the correct rows in the grid.

1 not the same
2 to put off until later
3 a place where things are made
4 container for rubbish
5 the outer edge of a cricket field
6 a soft red berry

If your answers are all correct the letters in the shaded box will make another key word.

B The answer to each of these clues has a letter that is either not sounded when the word is read aloud, or not sounded very distinctly. Circle these unstressed letters.

Here are some spellings with **unstressed vowels**. Remember, unstressed vowels are vowel letters that are difficult to make out because they are spoken quickly, or are sounded very quietly.

separate   is often pronounced *seprate*
boundary   is often pronounced *boundry*

Some words have **unstressed consonants**.

dustbin   is often pronounced *dusbin*
iron   is often pronounced *ion*

A Copy these words. Circle the unstressed vowels or consonants and write a mnemonic for three of the trickier words to help you remember how to spell them.

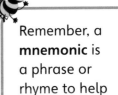

1 shepherd   2 voluntary   3 cupboard
4 parliament   5 medicine   6 postpone

Remember, a **mnemonic** is a phrase or rhyme to help you remember a spelling.

B Write the two homophones **stationary** and **stationery** in your book. Next to each write a sentence to show what the word means. The mnemonic 'buy stationery from a stationer' might help you.

Extension

It can sometimes help to spell words that have unstressed vowels correctly if we think of the syllables. Remember, a syllable needs a vowel.

separate   se / pa / rate

This reminds us not to spell the word *seprate*.

A Copy each of these words into your book, saying them aloud as you do. Next to each one write its syllables. The first one is done to help you.

1 frightening   *frigh / ten / ing*   2 business   3 prosperous
4 miniature   5 compromise   6 company   7 voluntary

B Use a dictionary to help you spot the unstressed vowels that have been left out of these words. Write them correctly in your book.

1 desprate   2 avrage   3 misrable
4 refrence   5 intresting   6 marvllous

tricky words 2

cough   suggestion   harass   communicate
thoughtful   recommend   embarrass

Focus

Key Words

committee
communicate
correspondence
embarrass
guarantee
harass
recommend
occupation
occur
programme
suggestion
immediate
community

rough
enough
cough
dough
although
bought
brought
thoughtful
plough

The key words are all tricky either because they have **double letters** or because they have the **ough** letter pattern that can represent several different sounds.

A List all the **double letter words** and all the **ough** words you can find hidden in the box. There are 13 words in total.

g	o	c	c	u	r	d	h	v	b	s	q
u	q	w	e	a	s	z	a	x	c	g	y
a	a	e	m	b	a	r	r	a	s	s	r
r	d	m	f	o	g	h	a	y	u	b	e
a	e	n	o	u	g	h	s	g	g	j	c
n	c	o	u	g	h	q	s	z	g	v	o
t	o	u	g	h	c	f	t	y	e	s	m
e	v	g	s	t	c	h	c	h	s	g	m
e	t	c	o	m	m	u	n	i	t	y	e
f	f	o	c	c	u	p	a	t	i	o	n
d	h	y	z	j	d	v	s	j	o	c	d
i	m	m	e	d	i	a	t	e	n	v	b

B Write a sentence that includes at least one word from each list.

What am I?
Match a word in the box with each of the clues.

> aggressive   necessary   attached   embarrassed   committee
> occur   excellent   correspondence   profession   apprentice

1 I'm another word for 'fixed'.

2 I'm a group of people who meet together to organise something.

3 I'm likely to attack.

4 I am a way of communicating.

5 I'm a bit shy.

6 I'm really good.

7 I'm another word for 'happen'.

8 I am a job that needs many years of training.

9 I'm a young person learning a trade.

10 I'm another word for 'essential'.

In each of these words one of the letters should have been doubled or one of the doubled letters should have been a single letter.
Write the words correctly in your book.

Use a dictionary to help you.

1 recomend   2 oporrtunity   3 marvelous

4 intterupt   5 esppecialy   6 equiped

7 exagerate   8 emmbarass   9 coresspond

10 comunicate   11 acordding   12 acommodation

geography and history words

castle

settlement

country

Focus

Look at these pictures. Select and write a key word that matches each one.

Key Words

castle
parliament
government
document
revolution
longitude
latitude
ocean
peninsular
island
location
settlement
county
country
archaeology

1 _____

2 _____

3 _____

4 _____

5 _____

6 _____

7 _____

8 _____

9 _____

These history words contain common misspellings.
Write them correctly in your book.

1 independance   2 defense   3 arceology

4 parlament   5 goverment   6 emmegrasion

7 riegn   8 seige   9 medievil

When you have
finished, check your
answers in a dictionary.

Extension

A Match a word from the box to each of these definitions.

> volcano   atlas   estuary   longitude
> contour   settlement   landscape   erosion

1 a book of maps
2 a line on a map marking points of equal height
3 a gradual wearing away
4 the mouth of a river, where it enters the sea
5 a wide view of the countryside
6 a mountain formed from molten rock emerging
   from deep in the earth
7 a place where people decide to live together
8 the distance of a place east or west of Greenwich

B Copy each of these words in turn, writing a simple
definition next to each. Use a dictionary to help you.

1 latitude   2 urban   3 amenity

4 climate   5 constitution   6 colony

7 propaganda   8 immigration   9 emigration

ent
ence
ant
ance

Sil**ent** eleph**ant**
Obedi**ent** eleph**ant**
Intellig**ent** eleph**ant**
Dist**ant** eleph**ant**

Key Words

silent
silence
exist
existence
evident
evidence
violent
violence
sentence
different
difference
distant
distance
important
importance
assistant
assistance
relevant
relevance
nuisance
restaurant

Focus

A Copy these sentences into your book.
Add the missing endings.

1 There was no noise. It was totally sil_____.

2 The police said they could find no evid_____.

3 This argument won't be settled by viol_____.

4 We will be going to a differ_____ school next year.

5 The shop assist_____ was very helpful.

6 Her discovery was of great import_____.

7 Every sent_____ starts with a capital letter.

B Write your own sentence using **convenient**
and **convenience**.

A Match these adjectives with their nouns.
Write them in your book.

adjectives	nouns
distant	sufficiency
sufficient	assistance
hinder	elegance
innocent	ignorance
obedient	intelligence
ignorant	obedience
intelligent	innocence
elegant	hindrance
assistant	distance

B Make a noun from each of these adjectives.
Write them in your book.

1 important   2 fragrant   3 absent   4 evident

5 convenient   6 excellent   7 abundant   8 different

Extension

Adverbs often describe actions.
Many adverbs are made by adding **ly** to a noun,
like this:

efficient + **ly** = efficiently

Remember,
an **adverb**
usually
describes
a **verb**.

A Copy these into your book. Add **ent** or **ant** to each one
to make an adjective.

1 effici_____   2 sil_____   3 import_____   4 frequ_____

5 abund_____   6 viol_____   7 intellig_____   8 innoc_____

B Make an adverb from each adjective you made in **A**.
Write a phrase or short sentence using each of
these adverbs.
The first one is done to help you.

1 *efficient*   *efficiently*   *He worked efficiently and had soon finished.*

Check-up 1

Focus

What are these? Write the words in your book.

1 two _____ 2 three _____ 3 five _____ 4 two _____

5 two w_____ 6 three _____ 7 t_____ 8 p_____

9 h_____ 10 l_____ 11 e_____ 12 d_____

13 g_____ 14 y_____ 15 c_____ 16 v_____

17 d_____ 18 d_____ 19 i_____ 20 p_____

Extension

A Write the plural form of each of these nouns.

1 shoe   2 berry   3 knife   4 kiss   5 donkey
6 cactus   7 sheep   8 cello   9 woman   10 phenomenon

B Add the prefix **im** to these roots.

1 possible   2 migrate   3 mortal   4 mature   5 movable

C Add the suffixes **able** or **ible** to each of these words.

1 sense   2 change   3 love   4 response   5 cure

D Add these suffixes to these words.

1 marry + age   2 funny + ly   3 stormy + er   4 happy + ly
5 necessary + ly   6 duty + ful   7 joy + full   8 thought + full

E Write the words correctly in your book.

1 alfabet   2 dolfin   3 geografy   4 pamflet   5 elefant

F Copy these words and circle the unstressed vowels or consonants.

1 definitely   2 cupboard   3 parliament   4 medicine   5 miniature

G These words are misspelt. Write them correctly.

1 exagerate   2 interuption   3 embarass   4 acommadation   5 equiped

H Make a noun from each of these adjectives.

1 innocent   2 assistant   3 obedient   4 absent   5 ignorant

silent letters

Key Words

thumb
subtle
debt

solemn
autumn
column

castle
listen
mortgage

knight
kneel
knuckle

wreckage
wrinkle
swordfish
answer

scenery
scissors

resign
designer

scenery

column

swordfish

answer

knight

scissors

Focus

There are silent letters in some English words because over hundreds of years the way we pronounce these words has changed, though the spellings haven't! The spellings give us a clue as to how the word was probably spoken in medieval times.

knight   **h**our

A Look at the key words. Which letter most often comes immediately before or after each of these letters when they are 'silent'?

1 w   2 g   3 w   4 c   5 k   6 t

B Copy three words that follow the pattern you have noticed for each answer in **A**.

A What's the hidden word?
Copy this grid carefully into your book.
Fill in the words by answering the clues.
Each answer is a key word.

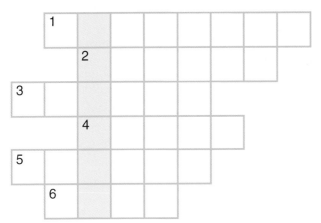

Use a ruler when copying the grid.

1 its plural is the same as its singular

2 the season after summer

3 to leave a job or team

4 one on each hand

5 a block of stone or marble

6 to owe money

What is the hidden word?

B Construct a similar puzzle yourself using words with silent letters.

Extension

One way to help remember when silent letters are needed is to practise saying the words quietly to yourself, splitting them into syllables and sounding the silent letter, like this:

Wed / nes / day   *and*   sub / tle

A Choose ten words with silent letters that you might find tricky and list them in your book. Next to each, write the word again, but split into its syllables. Then underline the silent letters.

B Write a funny sentence that includes at least four words with silent letters.

useful connectives

NEVER THE LESS

Focus

A Hidden in the word search box are thirteen connectives. Find them, then copy them into your book.

r	g	b	e	a	l	t	h	o	u	g	h
e	m	e	a	n	w	h	i	l	e	l	e
e	o	c	t	d	h	e	s	i	n	c	e
d	r	a	e	q	e	r	v	r	d	f	w
k	e	u	r	s	n	e	w	s	w	s	h
n	o	s	e	r	r	f	p	e	d	t	e
m	v	e	c	w	h	o	e	v	e	r	r
y	e	t	g	h	u	r	u	e	a	e	e
o	r	o	h	o	w	e	v	e	r	y	a
n	e	v	e	r	t	h	e	l	e	s	s

B Copy out the key words that are not in the word search box.

Key Words

meanwhile
furthermore
therefore
however
nonetheless
alternatively
although
because
nevertheless
whereas
whoever
consequently

furthermore   then   however   so   nonetheless   but   because
therefore   and   moreover   whenever   as   with   meanwhile
notwithstanding   after   when   although   if   since   nevertheless
while   besides   whatever   until   yet   for   consequently
whoever   whereas   alternatively

This box contains some of the most frequently used connective words. Copy those that are compound words into your book. Next to each word write the smaller words that make it. The first one is done to help you.

1 furthermore   further / more

Extension

A Copy these sentences, using the words in the box above to suggest words that might be used to fill the gaps.

1 It was an unfair tackle but, _____, he was determined not to let his pain show.

2 We could meet at two o'clock or, _____, we could meet later back at home.

3 The elderly lady was slow and _____ was slow crossing the road alone.

4 He is good at poetry _____ she is better at writing stories.

5 Jahan was looking for the kitten in the house _____ Jade was hunting in the garden.

B Make three sentences of your own using some of the connectives that you have not used in **A** and underline the connective you have used.

homophones and near homophones

The ball he **threw** went **through** the window!

Focus

A Look at these picture clues.
Write a matching key word for each in your book.

1 _____

2 _____

3 _____

4 _____

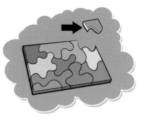

5 _____

6 _____

B Write a homophone for each of these words.

| 1 herd | 2 led | 3 guest | 4 cereal |
| 5 farther | 6 symbol | 7 lightening | 8 queue |

Some pairs of words are not actually homophones although they sound very similar and can cause confusion.

bought   brought

I **bought** some apples at the shop.
I **brought** them home with me.

Remember, **homophones** are words that sound the same but are spelt differently and have different meanings.

A Write sentences to show that you know the difference between these often confused words.

1 are   our   2 who's   whose   3 quite   quiet
4 choose   chose   5 loose   lose   6 conscience   conscious

B These homophones cause more problems than most.
Write one sentence for each set that includes each of the three words.

1 to   too   two   2 there   their   they're

Extension

There is a small group of words that cause confusion, though there is a fairly easy way to remember how to spell them correctly.

advise   advice   devise   device   practise   practice   license   licence

The words advise, devise, practise and license are all verbs, so can have **ing** or **ed** added, whereas advice, device, practice and licence are nouns, so can't have the **ing** or **ed** suffix added.

We have been **devising** a **device** to stop squirrels eating the bird food.

          ↑   ↑

       verb   noun

(action word)   (naming word)

A Write a sentence for each of these words.

1 licence   2 practising   3 advice   4 devised   5 practice

B Copy these words and write the definition.

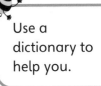

Use a dictionary to help you.

1 complement   2 compliment   3 eliminate
4 illuminate   5 affect   6 effect

er ar or endings

Who's the most popul**ar** football**er?**

Focus

A Match the words from the box to the pictures below.

| builder | actor | teacher |
| doctor | sailor | driver |

1 _____

2 _____

3 _____

4 _____

5 _____

6 _____

B Look at the final two letters in your answers in **A**. Sort them into two groups.

C Write a sentence that includes at least one word ending in **er** and one word ending in **or**.

Copy these sentences into your book.
Choose a key word to fill each gap.

My parents said they would buy me a _____ to help with
my schoolwork. As they are so expensive we looked for
second-hand ones in the _____.

"Is there a _____ type you want?" asked Dad.

"No, but laptops are very _____ amongst my friends,"
I said. "Look, this one has a built-in _____ to give the date
and a _____ to help with my maths homework!"

"I'm not sure about that," replied Mum, "but they are good.
It is _____ to the one I use at work."

Extension

Arrange these groups of words in alphabetical order.

1 instructor	instruct	instruction	instructed	instructing
2 circular	circle	circled	circulation	circling
3 computer	compute	computation	computerise	computed
4 popular	popularise	population	populated	populate
5 calculator	calculation	calculate	calculating	calculated
6 customer	customise	customising	customers	custom

ery ary ory endings

The st**ory** of Pirate McTrick**ery**
Is an extraordin**ary** myst**ery**.
He stole the stash
Both jewell**ery** and cash!
Could this be a major discov**ery**?

Key Words

mystery
discovery
jewellery

necessary
ordinary
dictionary
secretary
library
burglary

story
factory
memory
history
victory

Focus

A In the puzzle box, find three words with each of these endings:

ery   ary   ory

Write them in your book.

b	u	r	g	l	a	r	y	s
m	y	s	t	e	r	y	x	e
v	n	u	r	s	e	r	y	c
i	m	e	m	o	r	y	z	r
c	r	o	c	k	e	r	y	e
t	l	i	b	r	a	r	y	t
o	h	i	s	t	o	r	y	a
r	f	a	c	t	o	r	y	r
y	l	m	e	s	t	o	r	y

B In your book, write and illustrate a fun sentence that uses at least three of the words you found in **A**.

A Finish these words by adding **ory**, **ary** or **ery** to each one. Then use your dictionary and write a meaning for each word you have made.

1 hist_____   2 necess_____   3 diction_____

4 nurs_____   5 ordin_____   6 fact_____

7 machin_____   8 deliv_____   9 discov_____

10 mem_____   11 burgl_____   12 tempor_____

B Copy these words. Next to each write its root word. The first one is done to help you.

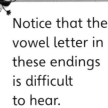

1 jewellery   *jewel*   2 machinery   3 bribery

4 observatory   5 discovery   6 nursery

7 slippery   8 factory   9 delivery

> Notice that the vowel letter in these endings is difficult to hear.

C What is the difference in meaning between **stationary** and **stationery**?

Extension

To make plurals of words ending with **ory**, **ary** or **ery**, remember to change the **y** to **i** before adding **es**, like this:

factory   factor**ies**   library   librar**ies**

A Write the plural form of each of these words in your book.

1 secretary   2 memory   3 victory   4 dictionary   5 nursery

6 discovery   7 burglary   8 delivery   9 story   10 mystery

B In your book, write sentences that use the plural form of these words.
You can write fun sentences, but you must include all the words!

1 secretary   burglary   dictionary

2 delivery   mystery   nursery

3 memory   story   victory

tricky words 3

communication

persuasion

equipment

Key Words

competition
explanation
profession
pronunciation
persuasion
communication

especially
incidentally
frequently
immediately
sincerely
faithfully

equipment
development
embarrassment

disastrous
marvellous
mischievous

Focus

The key words are all tricky because they have **suffixes** that can be misleading.

A All of the consonant letters have been removed from this word ladder. Copy the ladder into your book and fill in the missing letters.

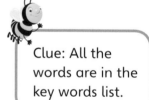

Clue: All the words are in the key words list.

			i		i	e		a			
o		e	i		i	o					
		e		u	e						
			e			e		i	a		
				o			u	i		a	i o
	e		u	i			e				
	e		e		o			e			
i		a			o	u					
		e		u	a		i	o			

B What is the hidden word?
Write a sentence using the hidden word.

Copy these words and next to each write the
root word to which it is related.
The first one is done to help you.

1 especially   special   2 competition

3 development   4 disastrous

5 mischievous   6 immediately

7 pronunciation   8 marvellous

9 embarrassment   10 sincerely

11 equipment   12 frequently

Extension

Here are some of the more frequently misspelt words.
Write them correctly, using a dictionary to help you
where necessary.

1 enviroment   2 temprature   3 vehacle

4 bargin   5 vegtable   6 desparate

7 compitition   8 explanasion   9 proffession

10 pronunciasion 11 pursuade   12 exagerate

13 oppertunity   14 comunity   15 curyosity

16 identety   17 contraversy   18 secondry

19 potental   20 loveley   21 necessary

British English or American English?

My *favourite flavour*

My *favorite flavor*

Key Words

centre
center
flavour
flavor
defence
defense
travelled
traveled
organise
organize
programme
program

Focus

A Use the words in the key words box to help you work out how these American words are spelt in Britain. Write the answers in your book.

1 fiber   2 theater   3 flavor   4 harbor

5 offense   6 leveling   7 color   8 canceled

B Write a sentence about the differences you have noticed between the way American and British people spell their words.

Many of the words where the American spelling is different from British spelling were originally French words. Usually British spelling has kept closer to the French spellings whilst Americans have changed the spellings slightly. For example:

flavour   flavor

A British words have kept the **our** in some French-derived words where Americans use **or**. In your book, write **British** or **American** for each of these words.

1 harbour   2 labor   3 humor   4 flavour

5 favorite   6 harboring   7 parlour   8 flavouring

B We are not always consistent when spelling words. Join together these root words and suffixes, but check your answer in a dictionary.
Write a sentence to explain what you notice.

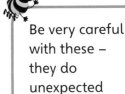

Be very careful with these – they do unexpected things!

1 humour + ous   2 honour + able   3 colour + ing

4 vigour + ous   5 vapour + ise   6 honour + ary

7 discolour + ation   8 invigour + ate   9 humour + ist

Copy these sentences, changing any American spellings to the British versions, as we would write them.

We went to the theater and first saw an incredibly humorous comedian with a gray, curly mustache.
We all thought his act was marvelous.
Second on the program was an aging pop star, dripping in cheap jewelry, who had traveled from New York to sing.
Dad said he thought her voice was dreadful, and her dress didn't look as good as his old, colored pajamas!
"I hope they improve the caliber of their performers or I'm in favor of canceling the tickets we have bought for next month," he added.
"Where's your sense of humor gone?" joked Mum.

a + double letters

A c**ann**er exceedingly c**ann**y
One morning remarked to his gr**ann**y,
A c**ann**er can can
Anything that he can,
But a c**ann**er can't can
a can, can he?

Focus

A Match a key word to each of these pictures.

1 all_____

2 att_____

3 ass_____

4 app_____

5 app_____

6 arr_____

B Write sentences using two of these words.

Hidden in the wordsearch are answers to these riddles.
Write the answers in your book.

1 Take off **ap** and you have a fruit.

2 Drop **a t** and **ion** and you have something for camping.

3 A small pin is the last part of this word.

4 The front of this word (that ends with **y**) is another name for a donkey.

5 The end of this word is the opposite of high.

6 If you're tired you'll like the last four letters of this word.

7 The last three letters are a tiny creature.

8 This happens every year.

a	n	n	i	v	e	r	s	a	r	y
t	a	c	a	t	t	a	c	k	f	z
t	b	a	s	s	i	s	t	a	n	t
e	x	p	s	a	d	w	e	f	z	r
n	q	p	e	l	m	a	c	e	d	l
t	o	e	m	l	a	r	r	e	s	t
i	p	a	b	o	q	z	l	t	v	u
o	w	r	l	w	d	f	y	q	r	l
n	p	z	y	x	e	u	a	b	e	x

Extension

Remember, a syllable is a part of a word that can be said by itself.
Each syllable has its own vowel sound, like this:

annoy is pronounced **an / noy**, so it has two syllables.
attention is pronounced **at / ten / tion**, so it has three syllables.

Copy the words below. Copy them into lists of one-syllable, two-syllable and three-syllable words, like this:

Does each of your syllables have a vowel sound?

1 syllable	2 syllable	3 syllable
add	adding = ad / ding	addition = ad / di / tion

appear	attack	all	allow	assistant
assembly	annual	arranging	attempting	apparent

ie ei

Eight fr**ie**nds in a f**ie**ld.

Key Words

belief
hygiene
believe
field
friend
patient
review

receive
perceive
either
protein
freight
rein
forfeit

Focus

It is helpful to remember that **i** comes before **e** when the sound is **ee**.

    rel**ie**ve   f**ie**ld

But **i** does not come before **e** when following **c**.

    dec**ei**ve   rec**ei**pt

And **i** does not come before **e** when the sound is not **ee**.

    h**ei**r   for**ei**gn

Write the words in the box below in a long list.
Tick the words in which the **ie** or the **ei** sounds **ee** (as in b**ee**).
Underline those you have ticked that have an **ei**.

receive	field	believe	wield
weigh	eight	their	deceit
rein	chief	shield	vein
receipt	sleight	leisure	achieve

50

It is helpful to remember the little rhyme:

'**i** before **e**, except after **c**'.

However, there are exceptions.

A There are seven different sounds made by **ie** and **ei**. Copy this chart and use it to group the key words according to the sound made by **ie** or **ei**. The first two have been done to help you.

ie or ei sounds like	ie words	ei words
ee as in creek	believe	protein
ay as in way		
i as in bit		
y as in my		
e as in best		
u as in hunt		
oo as in boot		

B Add some more words of your own to your chart.

Extension

In all the examples in the chart above, the two letters **ie** and **ei** form a single sound, or **phoneme**. But there are other words where the two letters are pronounced separately.

cr<u>ie</u>r   d<u>ei</u>ty

Copy these words into your book, completing the gap with either **ie** or **ei**.

1 cloth___r   2 r___nforce   3 spontan___ity

4 cop___r   5 obed___nce   6 sc___nce

7 r___terate   8 med___val   9 homogen___ty

more
unstressed
vowels

Key Words

explanatory
environment
secretary
jewellery
poisonous
company
desperate
definitely
difference
voluntary
reference
literature
temperature

Focus

A Match a key word to each clue.

1 used for personal decoration

2 good books and poems

3 works in an office

4 describes a substance that can kill or harm

5 anxious with despair

6 describes services given for no reward

7 without doubt

8 a business organisation

B Use three of the words from **A** in a sentence. It can be a fun sentence if you wish.

Remember, **unstressed vowels** are vowel letters that we either do not sound, or we do not sound very distinctly, as we speak. Unstressed vowels can cause spelling problems because it is easy to forget them and leave them out.

mem<u>o</u>ry

Memory often sounds like *memry* because the vowel is an unstressed vowel.

A Copy these words. Circle the unstressed vowels.

1 necessary   2 boundary   3 ordinary
4 victory   5 factory   6 history
7 mystery   8 slippery   9 machinery

B Find the unstressed vowels that have been left out of these words. Write them correctly in your book.

1 abomnable   2 busness   3 defnitely   4 jewllry
5 categry   6 frightned   7 widning   8 intrest
9 messnger   10 vegtables   11 vehcle   12 solder

It can sometimes help to spell words that have unstressed vowels correctly if we think of the syllables.

Remember:

• every syllable needs a vowel sound

• when two consonants separate two vowel sounds, the first syllable usually ends after the first consonant

hospital = hos/pi/tal

This reminds us not to spell the word *hospitl*.

Copy each of these words into your book, saying them quietly to yourself as you do. Next to each word write its syllables.

1 separately   2 compromise   3 disinterested
4 preparation   5 memorable   6 stationery
7 parliament   8 conference   9 unfamiliar

tricky words 4

sacrifice
criticise
prejudice
privilege
language

soldier
vehicle
muscle
parliament
conscience
environment
temperature
bargain
vegetables
desperate
definite
average
government

Focus

The key words are all tricky because they have **soft c**s or **g**s or because they have **unstressed letters** that can be confusing.

A Match a key word to each word and picture clue.
Write the key words in your book.

1 The [   ] has a smart uniform.

2 Our MP makes laws in [   ] .

3 "I'll take your [   ]," said the doctor.

4 [   ] are important foods to keep us healthy.

5 The [   ] skidded on the icy road.

B Underline the letter in each word that you think some people might forget.

A In each of these words one or more of the letters have been changed. Write them correctly, using a dictionary to help you where necessary.

1 mussle
2 predudise
3 privileje
4 languaje
5 trajic
6 garbaje
7 acsident
8 sitizen
9 sucsessful
10 exsellent
11 spruse
12 advantaje

B Write four more words that have either a soft **g** or a soft **c**.

Extension

A In each of these words one or more of the unstressed letters have been omitted. Write them correctly, using a dictionary to help you where necessary.

1 solder
2 enviroment
3 temprature
4 vegtables
5 desprate
6 defnite
7 avrage
8 consience
9 vehcle
10 goverment
11 bargin
12 parliment
13 diffrent
14 cuboard
15 boundry
16 jewellry

> Remember, dividing words into their syllables can sometimes help you to remember the unstressed letters.

B Choose five of the longer words you have written and divide them into their syllables.

ICT words

laptop
internet
computer
keyboard

Key Words

computer
laptop
cable
Wi-Fi
electronic
hardware
software
gigabytes
internet
download
memory
screen
program
spreadsheet
virus
mouse

Focus

A Look at these pictures. Select and write a key word that matches each one.

1 _____   2 _____

3 _____   4 _____

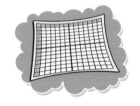

http://www.

5 _____   6 _____

B List the key words that are not listed in **A**. Next to each write a brief definition. Use your dictionary to help you.

Extra

All of these computing words are misspelt in a way that often happens. Write them correctly.

1 programme
2 ikon
3 processer
4 megabite
5 curser
6 disc
7 graffics
8 multymedia
9 daterbase
10 parsword
11 virrus
12 moniter

Extension

A The internet has its own language. Copy these words and next to each write what it means.

1 email
2 browser
3 cyberspace
4 domain
5 logon
6 newbie
7 icon
8 signature

When you have finished, check your answers in a dictionary.

B Spelling is notoriously bad on the internet. Sometimes this is due to keying errors but often it is deliberate to make keying quicker and easier. For example, numbers are sometimes used for letters, such as:

8 for **ate**, as in **C U L8R** (*see you later*)

Make up some spellings yourself using numbers in place of some letters.

tricky words 5

I would if I could but I **can't**.
I know you **wouldn't** so I **won't**.

Focus

I'm	I'll	I've	I'd	we'll
we've	we're	isn't	weren't	wasn't
wouldn't	won't	can't	it's	what's
	where's	who's	who'll	

A Match a contraction from the box with these pairs of words. Write them in your book.
The first one is done to help you.

1 I am = I'm   2 is not =   3 who is =   4 what is =

5 I would =   6 we are =   7 will not =   8 where is =

9 we will =   10 it is =   11 I will =   12 who will =

B What are these contractions short for?

1 I'm =   2 I'll =   3 I've =   4 I'd =

5 we'll =   6 we're =   7 isn't =   8 weren't =

9 wouldn't =   10 won't =   11 can't =   12 what's =

In each of these words one of the letters should have been doubled. Write the words correctly in your book.

1 accomodate

2 acompany

3 begining

4 acording

5 disapoint

6 embarass

7 aparent

8 apreciate

9 atached

10 agressive

11 hapened

12 posession

13 questionaire

14 sucessful

15 symetrical

16 patern

17 mariage

18 tomorow

Extension

Here are some of the more frequently misspelt words. Write them correctly.

Use a dictionary to help you.

1 enviroment

2 temprature

3 vehacle

4 bargin

5 vegtable

6 desparate

7 compitition

8 explanasion

9 proffession

10 pronunciasion

11 pursuade

12 exagerate

13 oppertunity

14 comunity

15 curyosity

16 identety

17 contraversy

18 secondry

19 potental

20 loveley

using a dictionary

GIDDY

giddy *adj.* dizzy, light-headed (comparative **giddier**, superlative **giddiest**). *adv.* **giddily**. *n.* **giddiness**.

gift *n.* 1. a present. 2. a natural ability.

do not look a gift horse in the mouth do not criticise a gift.

gifted *adj.* skilful, clever.

gigantic *adj.* enormous, like a giant. See **giant**.

giggle *v.* to titter, to laugh in an excited way (**giggling**, **giggled**).

gild *v.* to paint with gold paint.

gill 1 (*pron.* gil) n. the breathing organ of a fish or frog.

gill 2 (*pron.* jil) n. a liquid measure equal to one quarter of a pint (0.142 litres).

gilt *n.* a thin layer of gold or gold paint.

to take the gilt off the gingerbread to make something less attractive, from an old custom of gilding gingerbread at fairs.

ginger *n.* a tropical root ground to a hot spicy powder for flavouring food.

gingerbread *n.* a biscuit, or bread, flavoured with ginger.

gipsy see **gypsy**.

GLAD

giraffe *n.* a long-necked African animal.

girder *n.* a strong beam holding up a weight.

girdle *n.* a belt, a sash. *v.* **girdle** to surround (**girdling**, **girdled**).

girl *n.* 1. a female child. 2. a youngish woman. *adj.* girlish 1. like a girl. 2. belonging to a girl.

girth *n.* 1. a band round a horse holding the saddle in place. 2. the distance round anything.

gist (*pron.* jist) *n.* the main point.

give *v.* 1. to hand over, to deliver. 2. to pay, as to give a high price. 3. to yield, as the beam gives under the weight of the roof (**giving**, **gave**, **given**).

to give and take to be tolerant.

to give in to surrender.

to give out 1. to let it be known. 2. to run short. 3. to distribute.

to give up to surrender.

to give oneself away to betray oneself.

glacial *adj.* concerning glaciers.

glacier *n.* a slow-moving river of ice.

glad *adj.* pleased (comparative **gladder**, superlative **gladdest**). *adv.* **gladly**. *v.* **gladden** to please. *n.* **gladness**.

Key Words

letters
words
vowel
consonant
order
alphabet
dictionary
definition
origin
meaning
guide
abbreviation

Focus

a b c d **e** f g h **i** j k l m n **o** p q r s t **u** v w x y z

The words in a dictionary are arranged in alphabetical order.
Write each of these lists of words in alphabetical order.

1 horrible dreary commotion orderly stallion

2 argument analyse accommodation ambitious archaeology

3 claustrophobia knight collision knowledge continuous

4 deceitful descended definitely demonstration dealer

5 spruce sprout spring spread sprawl

6 interlude international intersperse interview interrupt

Dictionaries contain information about each word:

- its definition
- what word class (part of speech) it is (n = noun; v = verb; adj = adjective)
- its origin (in some cases)
- related words or sayings, if it has any.

> Dictionaries enable us to check the spelling of a word.

Use the dictionary pages opposite to help you answer the following questions.

A Write these words, spelling them correctly.

giggal   girarf   glasier   gigantick   gladest

B 1 Which word comes between **gilt** and **gingerbread**?
2 Which word follows **girth**?
3 What class of word is **giddy**?
4 What are the comparative and superlative of **glad**?
5 What is the noun related to the adjective **giddy**?
6 What does **to give and take** mean?

Extension

At the top of each page in a dictionary are **guide words**, which are the first and last word on that page.

Here are the guide words from three different pages in the dictionary.

IRON–JAR p115   JAUNT–JOUST p116   JOVIAL–KEEP p117

A Write the number of the page on which the following words would appear.

1 kayak   2 jolly   3 jealous   4 irresistible   5 jacket   6 jubilee
7 keep   8 juror   9 jewellery   10 juice   11 isthmus   12 January

B Copy these words into your book. After each word, write the guide words on the page in your dictionary on which these words appear.

1 foreign   2 embarrass   3 terminal   4 miscellaneous   5 outrageous
6 familiar   7 unconscious   8 percussion   9 jealous   10 glacier

Check-up 2

Focus

Write a word to match each picture.
Some letters are shown to give you a clue. Write the words in your book.

1 t_____   2 c_____   3 c_____   4 k_____

5 s_____   6 c_____   7 l_____   8 c_____

9 c_____   10 n_____   11 a_____   12 a_____

13 s_____   14 v_____   15 m_____   16 a_____

Extra

A These are compound connective words. Split them into their individual words.

1 furthermore   2 nonetheless   3 however   4 whereas   5 whatever

B Write a homophone for each of these words.

1 symbol   2 guessed   3 piece   4 lead   5 lightning

C Write a sentence that includes these three words.

to   too   two

D Finish these words by adding **ory**, **ary** or **ery** to each one.

1 necess____   2 diction____   3 ordin____   4 machin____   5 mem____

E Write the root word for each of these words.

1 especially   2 disastrous   3 marvellous   4 competition   5 equipment

F Write the British spelling of these American-spelt words.

1 center   2 flavor   3 defense   4 traveled   5 organize
6 theater   7 harbor   8 laboring   9 favorite   10 canceled

G Write the syllables for each of these words.

1 appearance   2 arranging   3 apparent   4 annual   5 assembly

H Add the missing **ie** or **ei** to spell each of these words correctly.

1 bel____f   2 perc____ve   3 fr____nd   4 rec____ve   5 forf____t

I Copy the words. Circle the unstressed vowels.

1 necessary   2 ordinary   3 temperature   4 business   5 interesting

J In each of these words one of the letters should have been doubled. Write the words correctly.

1 accomodate   2 begining   3 disapointment   4 aparently   5 symetrical
6 mariage   7 sucessful   8 atached   9 necesarily 10 agressive

Extension

A Write a sentence for each of these words to demonstrate their meaning.

   1 devise   **2** device   **3** practise   **4** practice

B Arrange these groups of words in alphabetical order.

   1 instructor   instruct   instruction   instructed   instructing
   2 computer   compute   computation   computerise   computing

C Write the plural form of each of these words.

   1 dictionary   **2** victory   **3** memory   **4** secretary   **5** nursery

D Write these misspelt words correctly.

   1 enviroment   **2** temprature   **3** desparate   **4** compitition   **5** proffession
   6 pursuade   **7** oppertunity   **8** secondry   **9** potental   **10** lovly

E Copy these words into your book, completing the gap with either **ie** or **ei**.

   1 med___val   **2** r___nforce   **3** sc___nce   **4** r___terate   **5** obed___nce

F Do these word sums.

   1 response + ible =   **2** cure + able =   **3** sense + ible =

G In each of these words one or more of the letters have been changed. Write them correctly.

   1 languaje   **2** trajic   **3** acsident   **4** sucsesful   **5** exellent
   6 megabite   **7** cursar   **8** viros   **9** graffics   **10** multymedia